November 8, 2004—Reporter Anne Garrels shivered on the bare desert ground. Her head was propped on a backpack stuffed with radio equipment. Above her, mortar shells whistled across the night sky. A gun battle chattered in the distance. The invasion of Fallujah had begun.

Writing Home

Garrels had spent over a year reporting on the war in Iraq. But she had never been this close to combat.

Just the day before, the U.S. Marines she was following had written or called their loved ones. They knew they might never get another chance.

Street Fight

Now those marines were creeping through the streets of an unfamiliar city, dodging sniper fire and watching for roadside bombs. Garrels had stayed behind. She knew she should be in Fallujah with the marines. But she wasn't sure she had the courage.

Moment of Decision

Garrels huddled in the cold and tried to decide whether she would follow the marines into the city. "How in God's name am I going to last?" she asked herself.

The Question

Why do reporters risk their lives to pursue a story? And how can they remain objective when they become emotionally involved with their subjects?

PREVIEW PHOTOS

PAGE 1: U.S. Marines sit in foxholes on the outskirts of Fallujah on November 8, 2004.

PAGES 2-3: A U.S. soldier writes home while serving in Iraq.

PAGES 4-5: A marine watches smoke rise from a burning building in Fallujah.

Cover design: Maria Bergós, Book&Look **Interior design:** Red Herring Design/NYC **Photographs** ©: cover top: Jonathan William Mitchell/age fotostock; cover bottom: Wathiq Khuzaie/Getty Images; 1: Anja Niedringhaus/AP Images; 2-3: Scott Nelson/Getty Images; 4-5: LCPL Jeremy W. Ferguson, USMC; 8: Lance Cpl. Thomas D. Hudzinski/U.S. Navy Photo; 10: Lt. Col. Jay Kopelman, USMC (Ret); 13: Scott Peterson/Getty Images; 14: Getty Images; 15: David Lindroth, Inc.; 16: Sgt. Clinton Firstbrook/U.S. Navy Photo; 18-19: Journalist 1st Class Jeremy Wood/U.S. Navy Photo; 21: Jim MacMillan/AP Images; 22-23: Khalid Mohammed/AP Images; 24: Cpl. Daniel R. Benn/U.S. Marines; 26: Lance Cpl. Samantha L. Jones/U.S. Navy Photo; 28: Capt. Scott Kuhn/U.S. Army; 29: Abdel Kader Sahadi/AP Images; 30: US Pool via APTN/AP Images; 33: Marco Di Lauro/Getty Images; 34: Roger L. Wollenberg/UPI/Newscom; 36: Robert A. Reeder/The Washington Post/Getty Images; 37: Cpl. Paul Leicht/U.S. Marines; 38: Rose Lincoln/Harvard News Office; 41: Anja Niedringhaus/AP Images; 42 top left: ID1974/Shutterstock; 42 top center: U.S. Navy/Getty Images; 42 top right: Wilfried Huss/United Nations Photo; 42 bottom left: Laurent Vander Stockt/Getty Images; 42 bottom right: Shawn Baldwin/AP Images; 43 top: Frank Johnston/The Washington Post/Getty Images; 43 center: David Furst/Getty Images; 43 bottom left: Scott Peterson/Getty Images; 43 bottom right: Fares Dlimi/AFP/Getty Images; 44 clothes: winterling/Getty Images; 44 recorder: Rtimages/Shutterstock; 44 phone: Jenny Matthews/Alamy Images; 44 battery: Robert Babczynski/Shutterstock; 45 money: Alexander Kalina/Shutterstock; 45 soldier: Jack Sullivan/Alamy Images; 45 wipes: Emilio Ereza/Media Bakery; 45 chocolate: Anke van Wyk/Shutterstock.

Maps by David Lindroth, Inc.

Excerpt from NPR® news report titled "Marines Plan Fallujah Assault" by Anne Garrels, originally broadcast on NPR's Morning Edition®, November 1, 2004. Copyright © 2004 by National Public Radio, Inc. Reprinted by permission of NPR. Any unauthorized duplication is strictly prohibited.

Library of Congress Cataloging-in-Publication Data
Names: Cooper, Candy J., 1955- author.
Title: Reporting from Iraq : on the ground in Fallujah / Candy J. Cooper.
Other titles: Xbooks.
Description: [New edition] | New York, NY : Scholastic, an imprint of Scholastic Inc., [2020]. | Series: Xbooks | Includes index. | Audience: Grades 4-6. | Summary: "Explains to readers how life is like in Iraq during war time"-- Provided by publisher.
Identifiers: LCCN 2019028969 | ISBN 9780531238196 (library binding) | ISBN 9780531243855 (paperback)
Subjects: LCSH: Garrels, Anne, 1951- --Juvenile literature. | Fallujah, Battle of, Fallūjah, Iraq, 2004--Juvenile literature. | Fallujah, Battle of, Fallūjah, Iraq, 2004--Press coverage--Juvenile literature. | Embedded war correspondents--Iraq--Biography--Juvenile literature. | Fallūjah (Iraq)--Juvenile literature.
Classification: LCC DS79.764.F35 C66 2020 | DDC 956.7044/342--dc23

Printed in Johor Bahru, Malaysia   108

SCHOLASTIC, XBOOKS, and associated logos are trademarks and/or registered trademarks of Scholastic Inc.

1 2 3 4 5 6 7 8 9 10 R 29 28 27 26 25 24 23 22 21 20

Scholastic Inc., 557 Broadway, New York, NY 10012.

REPORTING FROM
IRAQ

On the Ground in Fallujah

CANDY J. COOPER

■SCHOLASTIC

U.S. MARINES BOMB an enemy target during the Battle of Fallujah in 2004.

TABLE OF CONTENTS

ANNE GARRELS interviews an Iraqi soldier who was part of the U.S.-led coalition forces in Iraq.

1

Live from Baghdad

Anne Garrels reports from Iraq's capital as bombs begin to fall.

When reporter Anne Garrels arrived in Iraq in October 2002, the country was still at peace. She checked into the Al-Rasheed hotel in Baghdad, the Iraqi capital, and unloaded her gear.

She had all the tools of her trade as a radio reporter: a cassette recorder and three dozen tapes, a laptop computer, a satellite phone, microphones, and other radio equipment. She had stacks of books and articles about Iraq and a lifetime supply of Kit Kat chocolate bars.

The war was still five months away, but Garrels knew it was coming. U.S. president George W. Bush had been threatening to invade Iraq for almost a year. Following the September 11, 2001, terrorist attacks on the United States, President Bush had declared a "War on Terror." He vowed to attack countries that sponsored terrorism. Iraq, he said, was one of those countries.

Toughing It Out

Garrels had been sent to Baghdad by National Public Radio (NPR) to cover the lead-up to the war. It was a dangerous assignment, but that was nothing new to Garrels. During her 30 years as a foreign correspondent, she had witnessed wars in El Salvador, Bosnia, and Afghanistan. When she stayed home for too long she got restless.

When Garrels first arrived in Iraq, she was one of several hundred foreign correspondents reporting from Baghdad. But as the invasion neared, many reporters began to leave, fearing for their safety. By mid-March 2003, only 16 American journalists

ANNE GARRELS works on a story on the roof of a U.S. Marine base in Iraq. She reported for NPR, a radio station based in Washington, D.C.

remained in Baghdad. Garrels was one of them.

The Iraq War began during the early morning hours of March 20, when the United States, Great Britain, and their allies began bombing the city of Baghdad. In the days that followed, Iraqi police patrolled Garrels's hotel, trying to control where the foreign journalists traveled and what they reported. Garrels filed her stories at night, using a satellite phone she had smuggled into the country.

During the day, Iraqi officials took Garrels and other reporters on carefully controlled tours of the city. When she could, Garrels slipped away to speak to people in the streets.

In December 2003, Garrels returned to the U.S. and vowed to stay there. But as the war in Iraq dragged on, she felt compelled to tell the story. She returned to Iraq and traveled the country, filing hundreds of radio reports about the war's toll on the Iraqi people. For her listeners, the sounds of bombs and gunfire in the background made the war feel nearby.

Despite all her experience as a war reporter, Garrels had never seen fighting from a soldier's perspective. That is, not until Fallujah.

IRAQI DICTATOR SADDAM HUSSEIN was captured near a farmhouse outside Tikrit on December 13, 2003.

The Invasion of Iraq

In March 2003, U.S. troops and their allies invaded
Iraq and raced to capture its capital, Baghdad.

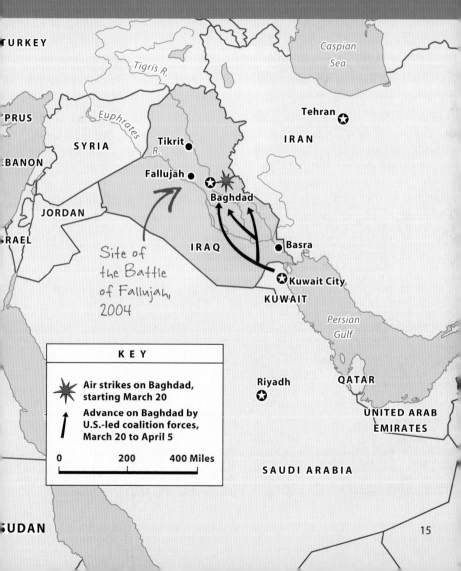

Site of
the Battle
of Fallujah,
2004

KEY

Air strikes on Baghdad,
starting March 20

Advance on Baghdad by
U.S.-led coalition forces,
March 20 to April 5

0   200   400 Miles

15

2

Road to Fallujah

The Lava Dogs get a taste of war.

At the end of October 2004, Garrels arrived at a bleak, broken-down U.S. Marine base a few miles outside of Fallujah. This city of 250,000 people lies on a main road west of Baghdad.

At the base, Garrels met the marines who would take her into Fallujah: First Battalion, Third Marine Regiment. Garrels had decided to become what the military calls an "embedded" reporter. She promised not to report information that might compromise, or endanger, the battalion's mission. In return, the military agreed to protect Garrels and granted her permission to observe and talk to the 800 marines in the First Battalion.

The First Battalion was part of a U.S.-led force that was preparing to invade Fallujah. The city had become a base for Iraqi insurgents—rebels who opposed the U.S. presence in Iraq.

Unlike the bombing of Baghdad, the battle of Fallujah would be a close and messy street fight. Soldiers would go door-to-door, searching homes for weapons and insurgents. The U.S. military had committed nearly 15,000 troops to the area.

"We Are Ready"

Garrels spent her first few days at the base getting to know the marines in the First Battalion. Based in volcanic Hawaii, they called themselves the Lava Dogs. To Garrels they seemed more like puppies. The battalion's motto was *"Ma Kau Kau,"* which means "We Are Ready" in Hawaiian. But most of the Lava Dogs had never been in combat before. Much of their training was in disaster relief and humanitarian aid. They had little experience with desert combat or urban warfare.

Just before Garrels arrived at the base, the marines got a deadly introduction to the war in Iraq. On October 30, a suicide bomber crashed an SUV loaded

THE MISSION of the U.S. Marines in Fallujah (below) was to seize the city from Iraqi insurgents.

with explosives into one of the battalion's trucks. Eight marines were killed and another nine were injured.

The following day, the company that suffered the casualties was given a day off to mourn. The marines gathered at the dining hall and talked about their friends. Garrels recorded them singing "Amazing Grace."

Keep Your Buddies Safe

A couple of nights later, Garrels sat with several men from the First Battalion. She turned her tape recorder on. So far it hadn't been easy to get the marines to open up to her, but as darkness fell, they seemed to relax and forget she was there.

Dennis Maguire, 21 years old, was cleaning his M-16 rifle of the fine desert dust that seemed to get into everything. He said he had never been in combat before.

"It's definitely the scariest," said Maguire, reflecting on the house-to-house searches that lay ahead. "You never know. You go into the wrong room…"

"We don't know if we can handle it," another marine admitted. "I mean, we ain't never been in it."

As the night wore on, the marines talked about the things that gave the war meaning for them.

"I love my girlfriend to death, and I love my mom and dad and my brother to death," said a voice in the dark. "But I can never be as close to them as I am to these guys. We live together, we fight together, we laugh and cry, we do everything together. We know everything about each other."

"It has nothing to do with, 'Oh, this is for Iraq's freedom,'" agreed Corporal Jason Hampton, a 22-year-old from Detroit. "It's just fighting to keep the buddies around you safe."

U.S. SOLDIERS in Iraq relax and share stories.

Live from Fallujah

Here's an excerpt from Anne Garrels's November 1, 2004, NPR story about the suicide bombing that killed eight marines from the First Battalion.

ANNE GARRELS: Over the weekend marines were returning from several days in the field when the company commander, Captain Gerald Garcia, saw a car suddenly come out from behind a wall of some kind.

CAPTAIN GERALD GARCIA: I looked into his face as I drove by. I looked at him, he looked at me, gave me a look I'll never forget and looked down into his steering wheel and then I—you know, everything came together—white Suburban, multiple bullet holes through the windshield, you know, the only vehicle sitting around anywhere.

GARRELS: As 35-year-old Garcia radioed to warn the rest of his convoy—a matter of seconds—the suicide bomber rammed into a seven-ton truck carrying several marines.

GARCIA: There was people jumping off of other trucks and jumping onto that truck as it was on fire and as it was melting. You know, with no regard for their own body and their own safety and pulling off marines that were burning alive. We were carrying our ammunition and pyro, so grenades were going off, rounds were cooking off. Marines didn't care, they just jumped up there. Our marines, they're incredible.

GARRELS: The marines continued to come under attack in what was clearly a well-planned assault. Help arrived, but eight marines were dead, nine injured, three of them severely. These marines have only been in Iraq for a couple of weeks. They were sent in specially to reinforce units for the anticipated assault, which will target insurgents' strongholds throughout Al Anbar province.

COLONEL MICHAEL RAMOS: You have to learn fast in this environment. Marines are great at learning fast and adapting to the enemy. Techniques, tactics, and procedures, that's what we're doing, and we're going to be ready.

U.S. SOLDIERS **assemble by a burning military ammunition truck after it was attacked near Fallujah.**

MAJOR RICK URIBE calls in the positions of insurgent targets in Fallujah so they can be attacked from the air.

3

"Sarge, I'm Hit"

A marine platoon patrols the streets of Fallujah with Garrels by their side.

Garrels and the Lava Dogs didn't know exactly when the invasion would start, but it was clear that it could be any day. U.S. military vehicles sealed off roads leading to and from Fallujah. Iraqi families were encouraged to leave, but single men under the age of 45 had to stay to prevent insurgents from trying to escape. Then U.S. jets and artillery began to pound suspected insurgent targets inside the city.

On November 7, 2004, the Lava Dogs spent the

day cleaning weapons, testing gas masks, and stocking up on ammunition. They wrote letters home and pored over pictures of their families.

The following day, U.S. military engineers cut off all power to the city. Artillery guns sent smoke

U.S. MARINES fire on enemy targets with an M-198 155mm howitzer. The artillery fire was called in by marines inside the city of Fallujah.

bombs into the streets to provide cover for the marines. Just after sunset, the invasion force began rolling into the city in armored trucks.

Garrels stayed behind in the staging area where the marines had gathered before they had moved into the city. She huddled in her sweatshirt for warmth and tried to decide whether she had the courage to follow. At some point during the night she dozed off. She awoke covered by a marine's poncho. She tried to return it, but no one would admit to the kind deed.

Into the City

On the morning of November 9, Garrels decided to venture into Fallujah. A supply train of armored trucks was making runs to the troops inside the city, bringing meals, water, and ammunition from the staging area. Garrels rode along for quick trips in and out of Fallujah. She saw streets full of debris but empty of people. Shops were shuttered.

But the quiet was deceptive. Insurgents hid on rooftops and in buildings, shooting at American

U.S. ARMY SOLDIERS prepare to enter a building while searching for insurgents in Fallujah.

troops as they tried to advance through the streets. The First Battalion had moved only 500 yards by midday. Six marines had been wounded.

Still, by November 10, the marines had occupied the city center, seizing houses to use as bases.

The following day, Garrels joined two platoons inside the city. The marines received orders to advance to a new house. It was only 250 yards away, but everyone knew that enemy snipers could be waiting for them. Garrels watched the first platoon lug their 75-pound packs into the darkness. They hugged a wall for protection and disappeared from sight. As the second platoon prepared to follow, a sergeant instructed Garrels: "Follow those two guys; they'll be with you."

"Okay, fine," said Garrels, though she wondered how she would keep up. Her pack weighed 60 pounds, almost half as much as she did.

Her two protectors took off, and Garrels followed, her tape recorder on and her eyes glued to the men.

Suddenly there was gunfire. "DOWN! GET DOWN!" barked one of the marines.

Garrels dropped into a crouch. An explosion ripped through the platoon—a roadside bomb or a rocket-propelled grenade. The voice of a young lance corporal rose above the din in a slow Texas drawl: "Saaarge! Aaah've been hiiiit."

AN IRAQI INSURGENT aims a rocket-propelled grenade launcher at U.S. forces in Fallujah in 2004.

U.S. SOLDIERS carry a wounded comrade to safety after their convoy was attacked in Fallujah in 2004.

4

House to House

The Lava Dogs lose two of their own.

The Lava Dogs responded quickly to the explosion that had torn into their ranks. The five soldiers who had been wounded in the blast were immediately surrounded by their platoon mates. The injured men were carried ten blocks to the nearest house occupied by the battalion.

Garrels rushed to the downed lance corporal and helped carry him to safety. A medic treated the injured marine for gunshot wounds on his arm and leg. Garrels stayed by his side. Heavy street fighting prevented help from arriving for hours. But the marine would survive.

On November 12, the day after the attack, Garrels moved to the relative safety of a command post. She learned what had happened to two of her favorite marines, lance corporals Brian Medina and David Branning.

"He Couldn't Say He Was Scared"

Medina and Branning were two of the more colorful guys in the platoon. The men had developed a signature style for the house-to-house searches. "They both kicked in the gate at the same time on every house," recalled Corporal Stuart Rogers. "It was their little call sign."

Still, Medina and Branning had their private fears. In a letter to his father, Medina had worried that he wouldn't come home alive. Branning had sounded anxious when he called his family before the invasion. "He didn't want to quit talking," said his stepmother, Tia Steele. "He's a marine, so he couldn't say he was scared."

MARINES break into a house in Fallujah to search for insurgents.

During the battle of Fallujah, Medina and Branning returned to a block of houses that they had swept once before. They searched six houses and found no weapons, civilians, or insurgents. They moved to the seventh.

"When Dave came in, he was looking up at the rooftop and the windows, seeing if there was anybody out there," Rogers told Garrels. "[The insurgents] had a machine gun set up right in the window of the living room. And when he looked up, it caught him right underneath the chin. Medina caught it shortly after."

Both men died. The Lava Dogs were left to cope with the loss of two more friends.

5

We Happy Few

At home, the wounds of war linger.

By November 13, the U.S. Marines controlled most of Fallujah. The worst of the fighting had ended just five days into the invasion. But the mission left some of the Lava Dogs with permanent scars.

Corporal Andrew Etheridge attended Brian Medina's burial at Arlington National Cemetery in Virginia. He was limping from a wound he suffered in Fallujah. Etheridge put his fists on top of the silver casket that held his friend's body. He laid his forehead on his fists and cried.

CORPORAL ANDREW ETHERIDGE (leaning on casket) grieves with Brian Medina's father at Medina's funeral.

"Sorry," he said. "I am sorry, I could have saved you."

Etheridge, 23, who had roomed with Medina, was nearby when the firefight that killed Medina broke out. Etheridge ran toward the scene, but he was shot in his right leg before he could get there. He blamed himself for Medina's death.

Corporal Alex Ayala also took the deaths of Medina and Branning hard. "It's bad, you know?" he told Garrels. "You lose friends, you see friends get hurt, people you love. You know their family hurts. So it's even hard to talk about."

The Costs of War

The Lava Dogs had thought their tour of duty would end within weeks. But another mission awaited them—providing security for Iraq's national elections in January 2005.

Four days before the elections, a helicopter carrying 31 service members—26 of them Lava Dogs—crashed in a sandstorm in western Iraq, killing everyone aboard. The disaster proved to be the deadliest day of the war for American troops in Iraq.

THIRTY MARINES and a U.S. Navy medic died when a helicopter like this one crashed in Iraq on January 26, 2005.

ANNE GARRELS RETIRED
from NPR after 23 years of reporting
from war zones such as Chechnya,
Bosnia, Afghanistan, and Iraq.

In past war assignments, Garrels was able to interview people openly. But Iraq was different. She had to avoid attention. She wore traditional Iraqi clothing and covered her hair. Reporters she knew were snatched off the streets and killed. Others were kidnapped for ransom. "We were worth money," she said.

Leaving the War Behind

Garrels reported on Iraq for six years. She returned home to rest for a few months each year. When she was home in 2003, she wrote a book about the invasion of Baghdad.

Garrels suffered a mild case of post-traumatic stress disorder (PTSD). PTSD is a mental condition that people can develop after experiencing terrifying events. Symptoms include nightmares, flashbacks, panic attacks, depression, anger, and sleeplessness. Loud noises often sent Garrels running into her husband's arms.

In 2008, Garrels's husband, Vint Lawrence, insisted she leave Iraq for good. She did, but she stayed connected to the soldiers who risked their lives in combat. Once after she had left Iraq, the mother of a troubled soldier asked Garrels to meet her son. Over lunch, the soldier told Garrels that he had witnessed an incident in Iraq that had deeply upset him. He couldn't shake it.

A Deadly Mess

Garrels listened without judgment. She understood. War is a deadly mess. The only comfort comes from the bonds that form with others who have been there. Garrels hadn't been a soldier, but she had been there.

At Brian Medina's funeral, the program featured quotes from great works of literature that had mattered to him. Medina's legacy to his friends and family could be found in a famous line from Shakespeare: "We few, we happy few, we band of brothers."

Garrels, it seemed, had become an honorary sister among those few. **X**

Timeline: Conflict in Iraq

1998: UN workers leave after claiming that Iraq had blocked their inspections. The U.S. and Great Britain bomb suspected Iraqi weapons sites.

2002: The UN orders Iraq to allow inspectors back in—or face severe consequences. Saddam Hussein complies.

1990: Iraqi troops invade the neighboring country of Kuwait and seize control of its oil fields.

| 1990 | 1991 | | 1998 | 2001 | 200 |

2001: On September 11, terrorists crash four jetliners into the World Trade Center, the Pentagon, and a field in Pennsylvania, killing 2,977 people.

1991: The U.S. and its allies launch a counterattack called Operation Desert Storm. They free Kuwait, but Iraqi leader Saddam Hussein stays in power. Iraq is ordered to disarm and to allow weapons inspectors from the United Nations (UN) into the country.

2003: President Bush says that Iraq has weapons of mass destruction (WMDs). In March, U.S.-led forces invade Iraq. (No WMDs are found.)

2007: Violence between rival groups increases. President Bush orders a troop surge, adding 30,000 more soldiers.

2019: New violence erupts at Iraqi-U.S. military training facilities. Non-emergency U.S. embassy workers are ordered to leave Iraq.

2010: On August 18, the last combat troops leave Iraq, officially ending the war one year later. However, the conflict continued. During the war, 4,475 U.S. service members were killed, and 32,220 were wounded.

2017: U.S.-backed Iraqi forces help expel most of ISIS from Iraq.

003 2004 2007 2010 2013 2014 2017 2019

2004: In November, U.S.-led forces invade the city of Fallujah to kill insurgents.

2014: U.S. military returns to lead airstrikes in the area against ISIS.

2013: Al-Qaeda in Iraq joins rebels in Syria to form the Islamic State of Iraq and Syria (ISIS).

2003: Saddam Hussein is driven out of power. On May 1, President Bush announces an end to major hostilities. But the fighting continues. In December, Saddam is captured. He is executed three years later.

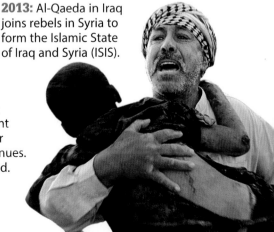

A Reporter's Tool Kit

Anne Garrels spent hours choosing what essentials to take. A reporter's "Go-bag" today also includes cell phones, SIM cards, car and solar chargers, satellite hotspots, and GPS.

1 Work clothes Garrels packed long, loose shirts and baggy pants to respect the conservative standards of dress in Islamic countries like Iraq.

2 Recording devices Garrels used a cassette recorder and a digital recorder. Reporters today also rely on cell phones.

3 Satellite phone with antenna This equipment, now much smaller than Garrels's, was used to transmit to NPR.

4 Batteries Car batteries were used as power sources when the electricity failed.

5 Spending money
Garrels traveled with a huge wad of cash—up to $10,000—strapped around her waist. She had to pay large sums for everything from travel visas to specific hotel rooms that had the best satellite reception.

6 Protective clothing
Garrels's gear included a plastic camouflage suit, helmet, gas mask, and decontamination powder to use against chemical attack. Reporters today also carry body armor, headlamps, combat boots, and survival blankets.

7 Baby wipes
Baby wipes were used for washing during the long stretches of time without running water for showers.

8 Chocolate
Garrels brought lots of candy because she disliked the food served in the Baghdad hotel.

RESOURCES

Here's a selection of books for more information about the war in Iraq.

What to Read Next

NONFICTION

Dunn, Joeming. *Fallujah* (Graphic Warfare). Edina, Minnesota: Graphic Planet, 2016.

Ellis, Deborah. *Children of War: Voices of Iraqi Refugees*. Toronto: Groundwood Books, 2010.

Martin, Claudia. *The Iraq War* (I Witness War). New York: Cavendish Square, 2018.

Perritano, John. *Saving Private Lynch!: A Rescue Story from Operation Iraqi Freedom* (Special Forces Stories). Broomall, Pennsylvania: Mason Crest Publishers, 2018.

Roy, Jennifer. *Playing Atari with Saddam Hussein: Based on a True Story*. Boston: Houghton Mifflin Harcourt, 2018.

The War in Iraq: From the Front Lines to the Home Front (24/7: Behind the Headlines Special Editions). New York: Scholastic, 2009.

Zullo, Allan. *War Heroes: Voices from Iraq* (10 True Tales). New York: Scholastic, 2014.

FICTION

Gratz, Alan. *Code of Honor*. New York: Scholastic Press, 2015.

Marsden, Carolyn. *The White Zone*. Minneapolis, Minnesota: Carolrhoda Books, 2012.

McCormick, Patricia. *Purple Heart*. New York: Balzer and Bray, 2011.

McDowell, Beck. *This Is Not a Drill*. New York: Nancy Paulsen Books, 2012.

Myers, Walter Dean. *Sunrise Over Fallujah*. New York: Scholastic, 2009.

Sherman, M. Zachary. *Heart of the Enemy* (Bloodlines). Mankato, Minnesota: Stone Arch Books, 2012.

Sullivan, Mary. *Dear Blue Sky*. New York: Nancy Paulsen Books, 2013.

GLOSSARY

ammunition (am-yuh-NISH-uhn) *noun* a supply of bullets or shells

artillery (ar-TIL-uh-ree) *noun* large, powerful guns, usually mounted on wheels or tracks

battalion (buh-TAL-yun) *noun* a military unit that is a subdivision of a regiment; it is made up of about 300 to 1,300 soldiers

casualties (KAZH-oo-uhl-tees) *noun* people who have been injured or killed in an accident, disaster, or war

company (KUM-puh-nee) *noun* a subdivision of a battalion, made up of about 100 to 200 soldiers (three to four platoons)

foreign correspondent (FOR-uhn kor-uh-SPON-duhnt) *noun* a journalist who is based in a foreign country and reports on events in that country

humanitarian aid (hyoo-man-uh-TER-ee-uhn AYD) *noun* assistance to people who are suffering because of a crisis such as war, natural disaster, or outbreak of disease

insurgents (in-SUR-jints) *noun* rebels who fight against their government or a foreign power occupying their country

medic (MED-ik) *noun* someone trained to give medical help during a battle

mortar shell (MOR-tur SHEL) *noun* a small bomb fired in a high arc from a short cannon

objective (uhb-JEK-tiv) *adjective* influenced by or based on facts rather than feelings or opinions

platoon (pluh-TOON) *noun* a subdivision of a company of soldiers, made up of about 16 to 40 soldiers

pyro (PYE-roh) *noun* flares, rockets, and other devices used to light up the night sky; short for *pyrotechnics*

regiment (REJ-ih-ment) *noun* a military unit of about 3,000 to 5,000 soldiers

roadside bomb (ROHD-side BOM) *noun* a homemade bomb that explodes when the target passes by; also called an improvised explosive device (IED)

rocket-propelled grenade launcher (ROK-it pruh-PELD gruh-NADE LAWNCH-uhr) *noun* a handheld, shoulder-launched weapon that fires grenades; also known as an RPG

satellite phone (SAT-uh-lite FONE) *noun* a type of mobile phone that receives its signal from orbiting satellites in space rather than from cell phone towers on land

sniper (SNIPE-ur) *noun* someone who shoots at others from a hidden place

weapons of mass destruction (WEP-uhnz UHV MASS dih-STRUK-chun) *noun* chemical, biological, or nuclear weapons capable of causing widespread death and destruction; also known as WMDs

INDEX

Metric Conversions

Feet to meters: 1 ft is about 0.3 m
Miles to kilometers: 1 mi is about 1.6 km
Pounds to kilograms: 1 lb is about 0.45 kg
Ounces to grams: 1 oz is about 28 g